Praise for Robin Marvel's *Reshaping Reality*

Reshaping Reality was very encouraging and spoke directly to me. It has helped me to be aware and let go of my bad habits and programming. I like to keep it's messages in my mind and it helps me to be kind and loving and to send good energy even to those people I don't like Reshaping Reality is a lifesaver."

~ Arnbjorg Finnbogadottir

"Robin comes to life in these pages a loving and gentle soul who gives to you the exact tools to do the same in your life and that is powerful. What I love the most is through the exercises and her inspirational guidance you find your own strength and power once again and that you Love who you are."

~Adele Marie

"*Reshaping Reality*, by Robin Marvel is an informative, heartfelt, and inspirational book written from the author's own life experiences. The message of this book is that in spite of an abusive childhood or any difficult life experiences, a person can change their thinking, their attitudes and their behaviors, thereby creating a better and happier life for themselves. The author includes many excellent techniques to release the past and empower the reader to attract a better future."

~Donna May

"I am glad that I read *Reshaping Reality*. To be honest about your life, to give these answers to those who need this information and will use it now is excellent. Being a man, I can only wonder what your life was like as a child and young woman. Now, you are a beautiful woman filled with positive spirituality, willing to share with people and help them find their reason for being here now. In my own way, I use your ideas to help people now, and am very grateful you put them into a book. Thank you again."

~*Two Feathers Reviews*

"*Reshaping Reality* is a perfect introduction for those who want to begin their healing journey from a traumatic childhood. It is filled with exercises the reader can enlist to step on the path of inner exploration to regaining a sense of personal power. I can recommend it for any adult who wishes to let go of a past filled with pain and trauma."

~Barbara Sinor, PhD, author of *Gifts From The Child Within*

"*Reshaping Reality,* by Robin Marvel, is easy enough to sit down and read in a day, yet I encourage readers to re-read different chapters later, after letting some of the information germinate. Robin's real life examples show that she has learned her lessons by actual experience. She shares her wisdom with us, of how she used these lessons to reshape her reality and how we can too.

Each chapter is followed by three exercises to help us look deep within our selves and integrate the wisdom from that chapter into our daily lives. Each chapter is brief enough to fit into anyone's busy morning routine. I'd like to use this as a morning refresher. I'll take five to ten minutes to read a chapter, review the exercises, and let the information sift through my mind throughout the day."

~Trisha Faye

"*Reshaping Reality* by Robin Marvel speaks truth directly into your soul. The love I felt as I read each page spoke to me in ways that you would have to experience just as I have by reading this wonderful, amazing, and very candid book. In Robin's simple, yet truthful words about her life experiences, she explains how you can take your own life back by looking within and loving yourself. Very powerful book."

~Anne Ford, host of *Connect With Your Guardian Angel with Anne*

"If your life isn't exactly where you want it to be, Robin Marvel's book, *Reshaping Reality*, will help you get there. In addition to reading her inspiring story, you learn, step-by-step, the little things that you can begin to do today to move your life in the direction you desire. Have a friend who is stuck? Send her Robin's book today. I was so into this book that I read it in one sitting. I truly enjoyed it and I expect you will too!"

~Wendy Merron, Wayne, PA

"From the very beginning, this book spoke universal wisdoms to me: things I know, and teach to my psychotherapy clients on a daily basis. So, read *Reshaping Reality*, and save on the cost of therapy! I think many people are aware of these truths, but we need constant reminders of them because they are submerged in the humdrum rush of everyday life. Most of us sleepwalk much of the time, and need a wakeup call to live deliberately and consciously."

~Bob Rich, PhD, psychologist, www.AnxietyAndDepression-Help.com

ROBIN MARVEL

RESHAPING REALITY
CREATING YOUR LIFE

Marvelous Spirit Press

Reshaping Reality: Creating Your Life
Copyright © 2012, 2014 by Robin Marvel. All Rights Reserved
from the Modern Spirituality Series
ISBN-13: 978-1-61599-111-2 trade paper
eISBN: 978-1-61599-877-7 ebook

1st Printing: January 2012
2nd Printing: January 2014

For more information please visit www.RobinMarvel.com

Library of Congress Cataloging-in-Publication Data

Marvel, Robin, 1979-
  Reshaping reality : creating your life / by Robin Marvel.
      p. cm. -- (Modern spirituality series)
  Includes bibliographical references and index.
  ISBN 978-1-61599-111-2 (pbk. : alk. paper) -- ISBN 978-1-61599-877-7 (ebook)
  1. Self-realization. 2. Self-actualization (Psychology) 3. Motivation (Psychology) 4.
Spiritual life. I. Title.
  BF637.S4M3676 2012
  158.1--dc23
                        2011053255

Published by Marvelous Spirit Press, an imprint of
Loving Healing Press   Tollfree 888-761-6268
5145 Pontiac Trail   FAX 734-663-6861
Ann Arbor, MI 48105   info@LHPress.com

See our complete catalog www.MarvelousSpirit.com

Distributed by Ingram, New Leaf Distributing, and Bertram's Books (UK).

Dedicated to all those with a story—I See You.

To heal internally, we must first acknowledge and heal the story we have lived as our reality.

Contents

Table of Exercises

Foreword

Most of us have gone through some type of traumatic circumstance—whether it be abuse, addiction, domestic violence, homelessness, or being the child of divorced parents—that has left us with negative imprints that influence our view of life and the world around us. And most of us know what it's like to have a dysfunctional childhood. Life happens, and none of us are perfect—not our parents, our siblings, or ourselves. The memories of those experiences govern how we live our lives….But, they don't have to. We can change. We can reshape our reality and rewrite our life script. If we don't, we will remain stuck. Unless we own our responsibility to make changes in our lives, we will unconsciously allow those imprints to shape our words, actions, and reactions so that our lives become a repeat of those remembered experiences, leaving us like a hamster on a wheel, unable to move past the pain.

We all have imprints, and they can be both negative and positive. Imprints are beliefs we learned early in life, usually in childhood, and often from our parents and community, or from an event we experienced. An imprint is a belief that shapes our thoughts and actions, a belief we often hold unconsciously. For example, if you are an early riser, you might have it imprinted into your thoughts that to sleep in is a sign of laziness, or if you were molested as a child by a church authority, you might have an imprint that no clergy members can be trusted. Those are examples of negative imprints—beliefs that are not completely true and hold us back from enjoying life or fulfilling our potential. We also have positive imprints. A positive imprint might be, "No matter what goes wrong, my family will always love me," or "Taking pride in my work is important to me."

The problem with imprints is that we aren't always aware that we hold them. The result is that we may end up behaving irrationally or in ways that prevent us from knowing our true potential. But, what we do know is that it's a choice how we want to handle these experiences and whether or not we want to abandon the negative cycle that actually leaves us stagnant; instead, we can choose to live our true potential.

The only way to break this cycle is to expose ourselves to the truth. The only way to break this cycle is for us to stand up against dysfunctional behaviors and show them for the untruths they are. That is the only way such generational dysfunction can be overcome.

Once we come to understand what our imprints are, we're able to become aware of when we are acting a certain way based on an imprint, and then we have the opportunity to change that behavior.

We can stop the cycles and move forward. We can draw boundaries about what we will tolerate in a relationship, or we can nurture ourselves by focusing on our strengths. We can define what our purpose in life is and set our minds to live that purpose.

We all deserve to live our authentic lives. Our negative imprints hold us back far too often. Discover and understand your imprints. It's time for you to free yourself so you can have the life you deserve to enjoy. It is time to reshape your reality and create your own life. It is time to break the cycle; it is time to be who you are. You've made your first step; you're about to embark on Robin Marvel's *Reshaping Reality: Creating Your Life*. In the pages that follow, I hope you'll find the courage to take the second step toward creating the life you want—and deserve. You do deserve it, and you can do it.

Irene Watson, MA, author of *The Sitting Swing: Finding Wisdom to Know the Difference* and co-author of *Rewriting Life Scripts: Transformational Recovery for Families of Addicts.*

Introduction

I wrote this book with the intention of shaking your spirit. I want to encourage you to use the negative situations you have experienced in life to propel yourself to a life of motivation and purpose! Let's face it; we all have a story ~ some of us choose to move forward; some of us remain stuck in a cycle of victimhood until we get the confidence to unleash our greatness!

As we each face the situations of life, I want you to know that you have a choice—a choice to become a victim of your life, experiencing each moment through the wounded eye, OR you can choose to learn from the situation and use it to propel yourself into a life of purpose.

This book is written from my heart. I can honestly tell you that I too have been there and I am here now, extending my hand to you. I am "That" girl the other girls talk about. I have been the child of domestic violence, a product of divorce, a poor kid, addicted to alcohol, a low self-esteem person, a homeless child, and a pregnant teenager. These are the life lessons that I created for personal growth and now appreciate the strength given to me from these circumstances.

I AM now "That" girl that chose to stop the cycle, who decides my own fate by making all the choices in my life, choosing to live life instead of being a victim of it. Each time I was faced with a negative situation, I made a commitment to myself to never settle, never compromise my self-worth. I have taken all challenges and turned them into motivation and purpose.

I want you to know that you deserve a life of bliss. Today is your day to change your direction, heal from within, and start *Reshaping Reality!* I believe in you!

Love, Gratitude, & Kindness
Robin Marvel

Stop the cycle. You are not the product of bad parenting.

You are not the product of your financial standing.

You are not the product of your social status.

You are what you choose to be <u>right now</u>!

Shake, Shake Your Spirit!

Are you stopped at the fork in the road, wondering which way you should turn? Perhaps you're being enthralled the ever famous questions like: Who am I? What is my purpose? Will it ever be enough? Are you following misguided directions, battling right versus wrong? Working to discover your *dharma*—an individual life purpose—will answer all these unanswered questions you have carried throughout your life.

The words of this book will lead you on your journey of self-discovery. Your story, my story—we walk as one toward purpose, strength, and confidence. We are now healing our stories, defeating limits in life, shattering the perceptions we have once known.

This book will motivate you to claim your power, a birthright for us all. As you start to read, certain emotions will be shaken within. Acknowledge these moments as a time to look within, and hear the messages your higher power is sending you. An initiative to start Reshaping your Reality.

It is time to make the choice to start experiencing life as an unwritten journey, holding the pen to a blank piece of paper, writing in whatever you desire and want, ripping out the pages of past mistakes only to remember the lessons we have learned. Today, you start writing yourself into a life of divine purpose, loving each moment, facing the unknown, looking your fears in the face and laughing as you gain confidence in knowing who you are; Reshaping Reality as you remove anything that may be limiting you, creating a state of joy, love, and inner peace.

Choice ~ The Right or Power to Choose

It is important in life to know when to adjust your direction, being aware of the stuff you need to leave behind, and what you need to keep moving forward.

Life is Choice

Life is made of choices. We have all heard this statement at one time or another during our journey. Our choices determine the successes and failures that we experience each day. The shaping of your reality depends on becoming aware of your choices and the effect they have on who you are. It is important to become accountable for your life choices right now, taking personal responsibility in the present moment.

Take time right now to ponder who makes the choices in your life? Are you stepping up owning your choices? Or are you choosing to be a victim of your life, finding excuses and blaming others for where you are today? Each experience you encounter presents you with the opportunity to choose a direction—the choice to learn and expand or the choice to remain a victim. What you choose creates your reality.

Have you ever contemplated just how many choices you make before noon each day? Just to start your day, you make the choice to get out of bed, brush your hair, and embrace the world another day. That is just to start your day; imagine the number of choices you make by the time you go to bed each night.

Recognizing that your choices create the day you are living is very powerful. It gives you the opportunity to be in control of your life without limits. Morning intentions are a powerful way to start each day in a positive mindset. You set your intentions each morning by being mindful of where your thoughts are as you start your day, only allowing positive, empowering thoughts to enter your mind.

For example, before you rise out of bed, state the affirmation "Today is a great day; I welcome all that comes my way!" Allow this affirmation to open a positive energy flow for you, setting the tone for your day.

Although choice is something we are in charge of, within our lives, there are so many situations that make it a challenge to believe you would have created it, such as: death, loss of employment, financial standing, divorce, inadequate parenting; and the list goes on. Questioning yourself in these situations seems the natural thing to do but the reality of it is that these situations are placed in our lives as powerful life lessons, chosen for growth and development on our path of enlightenment.

Choice has affected our lives since before we were born. It starts as we pick our parents in the blueprint of life.

I use to question the whole parent-choosing idea. If this is the case, then why aren't we all the children of famous, financially sound people with no baggage or issues? Instead, we pick and choose parents with issues of all kinds: abuse, psychological issues, and lack of parenting skills. As we awaken and learn more about ourselves, we are able to see the intricate part the parents we have chosen play in our growth and development. It is with this discovery we are able to release ourselves from the victim role created from our childhood.

Now is the time to let go of blame and live in the present, allowing the childhood victim to run free from our spirit. Acknowledging that our parents have been chosen for the lessons our soul has requested allows you the opportunity to grow and evolve. We are here in this spiritual classroom, having a self-created journey for the growth of our soul. This is a very real truth and it is the same for all relationships that are created into your life. Seems kind of harsh if your parents were anything like mine—drug and alcohol abusers who abused each other.

We are the people who really question this theory and until we are evolved enough to see the ultimate lesson, it is hard to believe this was a personal choice. Along with the lessons from our parents, we are given the opportunity to break the cycles. These cycles are almost endlessly repeated if you do not choose to stop them. This is proven all the time with statistics in life showing cycles that are not being broken; such as, a young woman who watches her mom physically abused and as an adult chooses relationships wherein she is also physically abused, creating excuses to stay in the pattern just as her mom did. I am here to tell you that just because a cycle is started does not mean it must continue. You always have the power to stop a cycle. I am not telling you it will be easy, but I promise you it is so worth it. It is a constant commitment to yourself and the reality you want to live.

As I experienced my childhood, I was quick to see that choices determine everything. My childhood was peppered with the lessons of physical and mental abuse. I survived countless nights of watching my mom being physically abused, kidnappings, homelessness, and drug abuse.

Although I was a child, I vividly remember thinking how can a person keep enduring the abuse my mom was choosing to live with. Every night my mom and dad would go to the bar, and I suppose it didn't help that we lived behind a bar; then they would come home and the fight would be on. No matter how hidden I was in the closet beneath everything I could find, it always led to the kidnapping of me and sleeping in a car, so my mom and the police were unable to find us. This happened way too much in my young life.

At that time, I realized the repetition in the choices that led to that same situation each night. I watched as the choices my parents continued to make were directly affecting my life. Although I was too young then to stop it, I knew I could change it by calling the police. Each time the police came, the fight subsided, at least for that night. And in some cases, I was returned to my mom.

Although I was unable to remove myself from the situation then, I know now that I have the choice to repeat learned behaviors or choose to break the cycle. I choose to break the cycle. I refuse to allow any abuse into my life.

Eventually my mom did get the courage to leave my dad. But she continued the same cycle of abuse. She entertained many relationships that resulted in physical beatings in the front yard. As a young child, I remember shoving my mom in ditches to prevent her from being run over by the abusive men in her life. This continued until I was a teenager. Not only was I fighting the abusive lifestyle my mom chose, but I watched all the adults in my life abuse every kind of drug you can imagine. It was no surprise to come home from school with mounds of weed piled on the table. It was a usual occurrence to see lines of coke on the living room table. I could have continued the cycle by becoming a drug abuser, but this is another situation; I chose to stop the cycle and live drug-free. These behaviors opened my eyes to how I would choose to live; how I had to make conscious choices for the life I wanted.

It becomes habit for so many to live life through the wounded eye of childhood, busy making excuses and blaming others for who we have become and how we are today. The list of excuses is endless: Do any of these sound like your excuses? *It was how I was raised; my parents weren't around; my parents were drug abusers; I was in foster care; I suffered abuse.* These are *all* excuses and it is up to you to make your life now. It is imperative to see yourself as an individual separate from the cycles your parents choose to live.

This is where active choice comes into play. Life gives us choices and that's part of the amazing journey. It is our life and no one or nothing can decide where we will go or who we are. It is your life; I can't stress that enough. That wounded spirit that was created during your childhood is no longer who you are.

Today cut all strings that tie you to your childhood and start releasing yourself from the past, breaking free from the cycle. Be aware of where you are creating limits based on the trauma of your childhood. Evaluate who you have become from the choices your parents made and now choose to reshape your reality based on who you are now. It is time to claim your life!

Exercise #1: Reshaping Your Choice

1. **Release Your Wounded Child** ~ Take a moment to center. 3 deep breaths, each time going deeper within, finding your inner child. See the areas during childhood that created insecurities and wounds. Explain to the small child you use to be that you are no longer held captive by the experiences of childhood. Embrace your inner child, wounds and all, sharing unconditional love. Repeat as much as needed

2. **Accept Responsibility for Your Choices** ~ No more excuses. You cannot blame anyone for your life. After all, it is YOUR life. Today's choices have nothing to do with your past. Each moment, you are responsible for what you choose. Take a look at your past and areas you are casting blame. Replace all blame with personal responsibility.

3. **Set Daily Intentions** ~ Each day, set intentions to replace the limits from childhood. Write these down on note cards and read them each morning. Carry them in your pocket or purse as reminders that you are in control. Live each day with positive, healing energy, knowing you are in control of the present.

Ego ~ The superficial conscious part of the psyche, developed in
response to environment;
self-centered egotism; conceit

Quit waiting for "IT"—You already have "IT"; You already are "IT";
"IT" is just waiting for you to open your heart and invite "IT" in;
"IT's" always been right there!

Let Go... My Ego!

Ego is defined as the superficial conscious part of the psyche, developed in response to environment. Look around at your surroundings; what are you feeding your mind? Our environment directly influences the size and energy of our ego. This leads to so much of our lives being lived through the perception of our ego. We each start forming it at birth and it continues to grow and develop through each stage of our lives, depending on what environment we live in. An ego demands to be the best, with no exceptions, becoming obsessed at times. There are 3 attitudes of personal ego, each one specific to where you are in your life; and all three attitudes working together create a life of fear-enhanced feelings within—of never being enough.

The first attitude is the need for approval. As toddlers, we await applause from our parents for everything we do. We crave a "good girl/boy" to validate that we are enough. This development of ego really kicks into overdrive as we start elementary school; we begin to be programmed that we must be the best—there is no room for anything less. We long for the pat on the back from our parents, teachers, any adult in our lives. We become overwhelmed with outdoing others at whatever the cost. Then we start middle school—the teen years—and the pressure increases; grades and popularity become overwhelming; all the while, your ego is developing strength.

The second ego attitude is the need to judge. Judging others creates a sense of power within us because it allows us the illusion that we are better than someone else because of what we have.

It is all about what you can show off: what car you drive; who's your significant other; are you popular; what brand of clothes you wear.

Your ego tells you that if someone else does not have as much as you, then they are not worthy. It generates a feeling of superiority. Ego attitudes are learned behaviors, a cycle handed down from generation to generation. Many parents have huge egos and are feeding their children egos by forcing them to be something they are not. Creating the illusion that if they hang with the cool crowd, only wear brand names, and make the sports team, etc, they will be enough and everyone will like them. So much attention is put into fitting in that the parent never finds out what passion really drives their children. This slowly diminishes their true shine, setting them up for a rude awakening as they grow up and reality sets in. When I was in high school, I watched the "cool" kids being run by the egos of their parents. They were taught to belittle others for not wearing brand names, walk around with intense arrogance because they were cheerleaders or on the football team, and just carry themselves as better than everyone that was not in their clique—a direct reflection of their parents creating a cycle. Now I see those same people living in the real world, and they marry people who they were mean to in school; they work in local gas stations and can't afford the brand names. It seems their egos were running their lives due to parental dictation, and now they have awoken to real life. You are not better than anyone else, ever. We are all divine and the sooner you see and accept yourself and others this way, the sooner you free yourself from the hold of ego. As we get deeper and deeper into the illusion, our ego continues to grow, as we are feeding it each time we display these behaviors.

The third attitude of ego is the need to control, to be dominant—to control all aspects of our lives. These attitudes become exclusively dominant as we reach our adulthood—we have to be above others, defining our lives by the illusion of "winning"; having the best job; the most drinking buddies; a big house; fanciest cars; name brand clothes; keeping up with the Jones' for sure.

Not living authentically because then, where would we fit in? The reason we develop this need to constantly strive to be better than everyone else is our ego-based belief that we are all separate from the whole. Not recognizing that we each are a contributor to the universal whole. We create a state of competition, feeling and believing that if we have the biggest, best, and most fantastic stuff, others will look up to us and see as *super-humans*—the all-amazing person!

These behaviors come natural because that is the way we know what we have been taught—a cycle. We continue to nurse our egos and they continue to get bigger and bigger until they dominate who we are and what we strive for in our lives. Don't be embarrassed; we all have one—it is bothersome, controlling, and sometimes downright overbearing. You know what I am talking about. We have all been there but now is the time for us to stop the cycle of ego.

When we are trapped in the ego mindset, we constantly live in fear and question ourselves. We start to wonder what else we need to be happy. Even with the cars, the house, the clothes, the better-than-you attitude, we cannot find peace and happiness. So we begin a mission of self- destructive beliefs that wallpaper over what's missing—beliefs like: *if I just have that job; if I just lose that weight; if I just move to a new area, etc, then life will be good.* It is all a mind game of the infamous ego!

The good news is that your ego can be defeated, if you choose; but it is a personal choice to start replacing the egotistical attitude with one of positivity and strength.

The reality is, it is only an illusion that influences our lives if we allow it. A self-created idea that you are what you have, creating better-than attitudes and arrogance. Choosing to live through ego, you have created barriers within yourself that are stopping a sense of fulfillment within. It is time to start being in control, removing ego from your reality; to develop a knowing that your happiness is only on the inside; and that the outer influences and circumstances that ego thrives on have no real place in your life. As you make the decision to defeat your ego, be prepared that it will not go down easy.

At each place that you are making the adjustment to remove it from the controls of your life, you will face challenges. The sly devil will always work to keep you living the illusion. This is the time to be strong, call on your true self, and outwit it. Once it is in check, you will quit trying to outdo others, and will find contentment inside yourself. You will start to develop a connection to the whole. The feelings of not having or being enough will disappear from your life. Today you put your ego in check by becoming aware of where it is showing in your daily living. Now is the time to reshape the belief that it is who you are and there is nothing you can do to change it.

I challenged my ego a few years ago and freed myself from the grasp of illusion. Who let that maniac run my show? Oh right, that was me! The choices I made to feed my ego were mine; the choice I made to cut it off was also mine. The power is mine.

As I was becoming aware of my ego and where it was feeding in my daily living, I really had an awakening of a lifetime. I was convinced that I had to have more—more of everything: a bigger house, a bigger town, a bigger life, all together. It was normal for me to live this way; I had been doing it for years—stuck in an illusion of *if only I had more.* It seemed as if I would be able to accomplish all that I wanted and needed as long as I had more, more, and more! I was convinced I needed this to be happy. Believe me when I say if you allow yourself, you will permanently live in an illusion.

I looked around at where I was living, and hated it. I allowed my ego to feed off of me by living with self-pity, blame, and judgment to justify who and where I was. My wings were clipped. Looking back, I can see I was creating exactly what I asked for.

I disliked my house; disliked the city; couldn't find people "like" me; my career wheels were spinning; and I couldn't believe this was my life. I was so focused on all I did not want that I could not see I was creating exactly what was there in my focus.

For me, it was always easier to blame and be angry with your situation than to face the ego and tell it to shut the hell up! I focused on the dead energy of the small-town life and negative vibes I was creating. Always questioning myself and wondering, *how can this be it for you? Don't you want more? Don't you know there is so much more out there?*

I was oblivious that the contentment I longed for was with me the whole time. Within me, I owned it but just couldn't see it. I was limiting myself in every area of my life. I just chose not to see it because I was so clouded by my ego-bound mindset. My well-fed ego convinced me that the only option I had that would make my life work was to move. After years of blame and resentment for this town, we moved.

Finally, making the big plunge... found the perfect home, in my perfect area; my stars hollow if you will (for the *Gilmore Girls* fans out there; you get what I am saying). The house was huge; the area was thriving, a big city with so much opportunity; finally free from the small-town living. Life was going to be perfect now! Two months after the move, I started being brought into reality, a lesson I no doubt asked for. So amazing how the universe will give you just what you ask for and then you have the opportunity to do what you like with it. You can learn from it, or you can make new excuses keeping yourself limited. I chose to learn from it, growing in strength and confidence. I looked around at this amazing house full of our things, full of our family, and yet it was empty. Our family, the most important thing in my life, started to change. Everyone started going in different directions. The connection that was so strong and important in Hersey became a thing of the past. Our connections seemed to be replaced with distractions. As we all were living these big city distractions, we were all longing to go home. But ego was not one to be messed with; more is always better. So the challenge to overcome this mindset was ever present, and it came down to me and what my truth was. I started to really evaluate myself and my expectations and my ego-based life.

The feeling of emptiness was a constant no matter how much I filled the house with memories, even painting it the same color as my small town house didn't help. I was constantly searching for something but just couldn't quite find it on a wild goose chase.

Then one day, it happened. Ego versus truth! The choice was made to defeat my ego. I stood back and looked at my life from the outside, and could see how I was limiting myself by trying to find my happiness in external things. Finding my truth within, I had to make the decisions to change my life. It was time and I was taking back the control of my life, my reality, my destiny.

I made a conscious choice for happiness. I had seen that all the happiness, security, and contentment I longed for was not in a big town or a small town but within me. Universe, are you kidding me? It was a knowing to move home, a simple decision that provided a release within; a knowing of happiness that I found living in the present, no longer looking for what was missing.

The simplicity and contentment I was so sure I made happen by moving were always there. Now I get it: more is not necessarily better. Having a sense of peace allows you to live fully.

Choosing to move home, I have gained an amazing sense of appreciation and happiness for myself and living in the now. A fresh new sense of contentment has allowed me to gain perspective in my life; to remove the ego mindset and allow peace, love, and happiness as a constant in my reality. It is actually embarrassing when I think back to myself letting ego run MY show, driven by the illusion. It has since taken a backseat in my life and rarely makes appearances, leaving me in control of who I am, living my life! It's time to fly. So let go... my ego!

Exercise #2: Reshaping Your Ego

1. **Becoming aware of where your ego is present in your life**—document where your ego is running the show. Keep it in a journal and as you conquer these parts of the ego, tear up the page. This will help you to know where you have removed ego and where you need to continue working

2. **Living with an attitude of gratitude**—Ego hates when you are content. Finding gratitude in your life will help to diminish the ego's presence and also enable you to feel good.

3. **Finding inner peace each day**—take 5 minutes a day and center. Tune out all worldly noises and focus on self and inner peace. Ego can't handle peaceful living; it thrives on drama.

Detachment ~ The condition of being detached; separation

The absolute truth of the matter is You are beautiful without the money, without the fancy car, without the big house, without the expensive clothes;
being who you are in true spirit shines beauty like nothing else.

Detachable Me

As humans, we find ourselves quick to attach to anything and everything—from people, to things, to words—assigning everything an emotion, a meaning. As you attach yourself to anything, you become dependent on it. We start to lose part of who we are as we allow emotional attachment to become dominant in our lives. It is in those times that our attachment becomes so extreme that our lives become intertwined, leaving emotions running the show. Although lessons are presented to us, we are unable to learn from the experience because we are so attached. If our friend doesn't call, we don't get the job; if someone calls us a bitch, we don't make the sports team, etc. We become devastated by the outcome. Our life is shaken and we begin to crumble. We give away our power and start creating a pity party as the guest of honor: Life isn't fair; they are out to get us (whoever they are); and the list can go on forever.

We function in our daily living based on the level of attachment these things and people give back to us. To detach, you do not need to give all your possessions away, leave your family behind, or go off the grid. Detaching is about owning your emotions.

The attachment to people can paralyze us in many ways. We can start to place so much value on the thoughts and beliefs of these people in our lives that we lose sight of our own worth. We allow ourselves to be mistreated because it is more important to have friends than to honor who we are. The amount of power we allow our attachment to people to control us depends on how we feel about ourselves.

People can only treat you how you allow them to treat you. If you carry yourself with self-respect, others will respect you as well. When you value yourself, it rubs off on others. On the other hand, when we have little to no value and self-respect for ourselves, others treat us accordingly. When we are unable to find value in ourselves, we seek that validation from others, making what they say more important than how we feel as a person. It becomes imperative that other people see us as important and allow us to become attached to them. The attachment of being accepted is a driving force in allowing others to treat us poorly. People treat you exactly how you allow.

Making the decision to detach from certain people in your life, those that are toxic, can be a daunting experience, and the most liberating one of your life. We each grow and expand consciously in our own time, creating friction as our vibrations are raising while others stay stagnant. Finding confidence and self-respect is the first step to detaching from unhealthy relationships in your life. As we choose to live consciously, we start to demand respect for ourselves from everyone in our lives. We no longer will allow ourselves or others to abuse us in any way. This includes family members—just because someone is related to us by blood or by marriage does not mean they can suck the life out of us.

For most people that have been treating us this way for such a long time, and know what they are doing, it is time to honor ourselves by detaching ourselves from them emotionally. So many people feel obligated to family. These are old beliefs that we must remove and no longer tolerate abuse from anyone including family. We must allow people to live their own way, but without letting it affect our spirit. Remove yourself from others that bring you down in any way. A great exercise to start stepping away from toxic relationships is to start saying *no*. When someone wants you to do something that is stretching your limits, say no. If you have a healthy relationship with that person, they will understand and honor your newfound confidence.

We also become extremely attached to things. Our cars, our books, our houses… okay, everything we own. These things become distractions from what is real in our lives. I am not saying you should sell all your belongings; I am saying that we can enjoy these things in our lives without developing emotional attachment to them. You no longer have to be so attached to things that your emotions revolve around what you have; so that when a book gets coffee spilled on it, you are able to keep your sanity because you know that it is just a thing. I have seen people lose all composure over spilled milk many times. This is all caused by the value you give these things. Make the decision to detach from things and start to live a healthy life. Know that things are just things, and in most cases are replaceable. Things are not what is important in life. You can look within yourself and you will know when it is time to release yourself from the things of life, removing the emotional attachment that is affecting the positivity in your life.

Do you remember the last time you were upset over something someone said about you? If you are like me, it is common to hear through the grapevine someone said something. Really think about how you reacted. This is an example of the attachment you hold to words. We are taught as little kids that certain words are bad, certain words are special, and certain words should not ever be said. This instantly adds emotion to words. We create meaning for each word, becoming attached to what they mean to us. So when someone calls us a bitch, we get upset, attaching a negative feeling to what was said. Now when someone says we are beautiful, we feel good, attaching a positive feeling to what was said. Words are not the culprit here; your emotions that you attach to these words are what have the effect on your person. The most freeing feeling in the world is to detach from words. When you can look at what others are saying to you or about you and still keep yourself centered, you are free from that emotional attachment. Do not allow words to have any power over you. People will say what they will, but you hold your power in how you feel about it.

Detachment is all about allowing ourselves to still be OK even when things do not work out the way we expected. Knowing that the opportunity to feel good no matter the outcome of situations you face in life is your choice. Although life may shake your spirit, and a curveball may come your way, you can take it in stride with a sense of knowing and maintaining inner peace.

As I started to choose to detach, I found myself feeling alone. As I started to change vibrationally, the people were dropping like flies. My attachment to needing acceptance was leaving me questioning if there was something wrong with me. Was I not a good person? Would it be easier to just conform to the societal norm? I also wondered all along whether it was easier to stay in this cycle of abuse or to be alone. These questions led me to really start contemplating my emotional attachment to the people in my life. I was allowing them the control of my emotions. Then, like clockwork, my eyes started to open and I began discovering the negative impacts they had on who I was as a person; how much of my power I was giving away by attaching meaning to these people; and how they saw me.

Then it became easy for me to detach. Popularity became something of the past, a high school issue left in the dust. I committed to myself and made the decision that I would rather be alone living with integrity and truth than attached to the need of being surrounded with toxic relationships.

As you develop self-confidence within yourself, you will find that you start to attract people who value your worth as much as you do. Your conscious self will no longer allow those that do not know you are wonderful to play in your game of life.

I have several people in my family that I love deeply, but I choose for them to not be a constant presence in my journey. These people are negative about themselves and life in general. It has nothing to do with feeling superior; it is because I honor my right to choose who is in my life, and I will not allow any toxic people to contaminate where I am living. I refuse to tolerate gossip, belittling, and meanness from others. And you know what, the more I honor this in myself, the farther these people stay from me by their choice and mine. Positivity intimidates negativity in ALL WAYS.

Exercise #3: Reshaping To Detach

1. **Recognize your attachment** to certain words, people, and outcomes. Create affirmations to detach from these. "I am Free from attachments to_____" Repeat! Refuse any toxic people to imprint their energy on you.

2. **Start small.** Focus on certain things you find yourself attached to. Come into the knowing that things, words, and situations have NO meaning unless you say so. Start with the next time you hear someone has said something negative about you. Look at the situation; laugh it off; and realize you are in control!

3. **Welcome new opportunities** into your life, but do not bank your emotions on them. If that job passes you by, you don't make the sports team, etc, you can be disappointed, but do not allow it to determine your emotional state; always keep your inner peace.

Truth ~ The state or *character of being true*

You cannot find your truth in someone else's illusion of reality. You must explore your true, authentic self, the inner self, and learn what is the truth for your reality. Otherwise, you are just going through the motions of life, never really living your life.

The Truth is...

Have you ever questioned your beliefs? I mean what you really, truly, deeply believe in your soul. We each live our lives through individual beliefs. All our decisions are based on what we have been taught. A majority of our beliefs come from outside influences, such as our parents, school, and society. Consistently learning these beliefs, they become programmed into our way of life. Our minds, acting like a computer, become programmed—input being entered from everyone around us and then computed as needed. Unlike a computer, our minds do not have a delete button; we must choose to reboot. Reprogramming has to be a decision we both make and follow through with.

As we begin to grow individually, walking our own path, we start to look at our lives and question why we believe certain ways, finding doubt in some of the methods we were taught. This allows us to become free thinkers and start to disassemble the programmed beliefs, our eyes wide open, discovering that beliefs we are living are not ours but in fact learned beliefs of other people. You start to open up to defining personal truths and beliefs. They are no longer a learned behavior but a personal choice. As you are living your truth, you become confident of your true beliefs, the part of you that really counts, seeing what works for you and what doesn't. Following others is just not an option anymore; you are finding yourself and loving it! Just because a guru or prominent figure says something is so, it does not mean it is your belief, or anyone else's for that matter. It only means that it is the truth for that person. Be diligent in keeping your beliefs very personal to you, all the while keeping your mind wide open to new truths and beliefs coming your way. We can always learn new things that resonate within our spirit. It seems to happen that when you think you know so much, life opens your eyes to so much more you don't know. When you decide to quit learning new things, this is when you quit growing and expanding mind, body, and spirit.

Becoming more defined with your true beliefs, you will discover people that make it their business to tell you what is wrong and right about your beliefs. There is no right or wrong in beliefs; it is all personal choice—an individual perception. Many individuals attempt to discourage others' truths and beliefs, based on their personal limits. This can present a challenge within you if they are unable to honor your truth. In situations that rock the truth boat, it is important to share with those opposing you that you honor their beliefs and ask that they do the same for you. Never argue that you know best; only showing respect for each individual's truths.

Look deep within and find areas where you are following old beliefs. This old, worn-out programming—from parents, school teachers, clergy—will do you no good now. This is a self-made life and you are the creator. Reevaluate your personal beliefs and see where they stemmed from and whether they are authentically yours. If they are not yours, let go of them and create new beliefs that are all yours.

In life, certain actions lead to indefinite labels due to old programming and beliefs. Some people refuse to progress forward in life and stay stuck with outdated beliefs.

It is taboo to be a teen mother. You are instantly labeled as a slut who will drop out of high school and live on welfare your entire life. Oh, if I had a dime for each time I heard this! I became a mother at age 17— the result of living a party lifestyle, looking to boys and alcohol for getting the attention I was lacking. The day they told me that I was having a baby girl, I made the decision that we would not be statistics. I did not care that the belief of society destined me to a life of struggle and unhappiness.

Not my life! I choose to live my truth and it made no difference to me what others had to say.

I delivered my daughter on August 20th at age 17, and I was at the Reed City High School on August 24th to start my Senior year. Of course the school district that I had attended since 7th grade was anything but nice to me. They made the effort to shove me into alternative education; they did not want their reputation tarnished by having a senior with a baby. I refused. I was walking that graduation stage with my class, like it or not. This made for a long, uncomfortable year with teachers, parents, and society frowning on my presence: how dare I break traditions by being in school with a baby! Many parents would not allow their kids around me because, of course, we all know pregnancy is contagious. The truth is their daughters were doing the same thing I was; I just got caught.

One counselor made it his mission to discourage and belittle me at every chance he got, conveniently missing that I was ½ credit short to graduate until three weeks before graduation. He less than kindly came up to me in the lunch line and told me I would not graduate due to the missing credit and there was no way I would make it up in time. *Oh really?* He sure didn't know who he was talking to! I completed the home study course in half the time and *BAM* I walked that graduation stage, head held high. Knowing my truths and beliefs were defined by me, not by a small-town high school, teachers, or parents that are so wrapped up in their outdated beliefs that there is no room for anything else.

Know that your beliefs and truths create who you are and can change and expand at anytime. Do not ever limit yourselves to what is suppose supposed to be—Create what IS.

Exercise #4: Reshaping Your Truth

1. **Evaluate your past teachers** (parents, school teachers, clergy, etc.); decide when their truths became yours. Are these learned truths deep down yours, or do they belong to someone else? If they are yours, keep them; if not, delete them.

2. **Do not sacrifice who you are** to fit in; know what your beliefs are and stand by them. Follow your heart. Standing up for what you believe in is important, even if it doesn't fit the mold, and especially if it doesn't fit the mold.

3. **Keep learning!** We are all in this life keep learning new things and it is when we stop learning that we are unable to continue growing.

Absorbing ~ To take in and incorporate

Energy ~ The power by which anything acts effectively

Your energy is yours alone. It cannot be imprinted by others without your permission. Carry yourself with positivity and strength, not ever allowing negative energy to affect you.

It's *My* Energy

Energy surrounds us, is within us, and is all that we are. You are seeing and feeling it at all times. A great exercise that will help you to discover your energy is Feel Your Energy. The way this exercise works is to rub your hands vigorously together palm to palm for about 45 seconds. Pull your hands about three to four inches apart; the friction you are feeling is your personal energy!

As we travel through our lives, we are consistently building our energetic profile. It is compiled of all your energy experiences to date. To fine tune your energetic profile, you must be alert to negative and positive vibes. During our daily lives, we swap energy constantly with everyone we meet. You get a little of yours on them and they get a little of theirs on you, absorbing the positive and negative of each encounter. It is up to you how much energy of others you allow to become a part of you energetically.

You make the choice as to what energy your profile carries. Your energy is your business; it can be positive, upbeat, and happy; or you can be negative, down, and unhappy—each characteristic determining the energy you are sharing with the world. You must work to keep your energy in tune, creating a sense of completeness for your integrated whole. A great way to keep your energy positively tuned is to exercise your chakras. Our chakras are the seven major energy centers within our bodies that are responsible for the health of our mind, body, and spirit. Every individual has seven major chakras that are approximately 2-3 inches in diameter and are in the shape of a circle, rotating clockwise.

They start at the base of the spine and continue to the top of our head. Having a balanced chakra system guarantees optimal health and a positive energy flow. An optimal way to keep your chakras in balance is to ChakraCize. ChakraCizes are a set of seven exercises that guarantee healthy energy flow, resulting in a vibrant mind, body, and spirit. I have included the seven ChakraCizes at the end of this chapter.

A major influence on our energy is other people. Who are you surrounding yourself with? Who do you allow to impact your energy field? Are negative people a constant in your life? The chakra system acts as a strainer that filters our energy as well as the energy we come in contact with on a daily basis. Remember that positive energy trumps negative in all situations. Be energy-efficient in your situations.

Although we cannot control the energy given out by others, we can always choose how their energy affects us. What parts of their energy we allow to become part of us. It is easy to become so wrapped up in the drama of others that we can begin to live with that energy, allowing the energy of others to directly affect our life.

If you choose to live in this negative energy, you will begin to attract and create your own negativity. You must be aware of what energy you are allowing to participate in your life because it reflects in everything you do and everything you are.

You are responsible for the energetic reflection you share with our world. Each time you are thinking a thought or speaking a word, you are creating energy and, in essence, creating your life. As you create this energy, positive or negative, the universe is sure to be listening and excited to give you what you are asking for. There are many distractions in your daily life that, if you allow, can and will affect your thoughts and in turn affect your entire existence. These distractions can be dismissed by being aware of what you are feeding your mind. Do not allow any negativity into your reality. Choose people, books, media, etc, that are upbeat, full of love and positive energy.

Do not expose yourself to negativity whether it is in the form of newspapers, books, television shows, or people. By becoming aware of the distractions you face, you are able to be in control of the energy you are creating. Choosing to experience positive energy, we can feel the connection to spirit; as we choose to experience negative energy, we become further from spirit. We will ask ourselves why we keep living this way; why is life bringing us these situations; but the truth is we are creating them. If you are living like just going through the motions, then that is what your life will reflect. Until we make the decision to eliminate all drama from our lives and pay attention to where our energy is, we will repeat the cycle.

You must be an active participant in your energetic life. Remove yourself from the drama of others by refusing to gossip. When your best friend calls you on the phone to chat about others, kindly say, "I love to talk to you about what is going on in your life, but I am not interested in chatting about others." This lets them know you mean business and drama has no place in your life.

Do things that build up your energy. Enjoy life by feeling the life energy in all things that surround you, like the trees, the birds, the amazing earth we live upon. This will not only boost your energy but will allow you to connect with *the now* moment of life, finding clarity and balancing your energy.

In times when I find myself overwhelmed with the tasks of life—bills, kids, and work—I will stop what I am doing and walk down and sit on the riverbank. I make it a point to center there for at least ten minutes. This slows me down enough to focus on what's important in life. I am able to reenter my life with my energy calmed and a sense of inner peace.

I also refuse to allow any negativity in my life. I realize that this life is a privilege, and I am not wasting one minute caught up in drama. I am responsible for my energetic profile and reflection that I share with the world. I take full responsibility for me.

Exercise #5: Reshaping Your Energy

1. **Be picky** about who you allow in your energy field. Invite in positive people. Remove negative people.

2. **Be responsible** for your energetic profile. Allow yourself time to really explore what enhances your energy.

3. **Refuse to gossip.** Let others know that you are not interested in talking about others.

ChakraCize Your Spirit

Root Chakra

The root chakra is the first of the seven chakras and is located at the base of the spine. The root chakra holds survival and security energy. This is also where your childhood energy settles.

When your root chakra is blocked, you can suffer from low self-esteem, living with a victim personality and acting self-destructive.

A root chakra that is too open has characteristics of being self-centered, a bully mindset.

When you have a balanced chakra, you will be self-confident with high self-esteem to share with the world.

The chakracize for the root chakra is the bridge pose. This chakracize will increase energy and circulation in your lower body as well as open the channels between your upper and lower chakras.

ChakraCize: Root Chakra ~ Bridge Pose

Step 1: Lie on back with arms at your side, palms facing the floor.

Step 2: Take a deep breath, bend knees, and lift your booty off the floor. Keep your feet flat on the floor. Stay in this position as long as you are comfortable.

Step 3: Lower yourself to the floor.

Affirmation: "I am Connected to the Earth."

You can use positive affirmations to enhance the results of each chakracize. Repeat as needed!

Sacral Chakra

The second chakra is the sacral chakra. It is located below your bellybutton and carries your creativity and emotional energies.

When your sacral chakra is blocked, you can have a lack of creativity as well as emotional outbursts. This can include writer's block and excessive aggression.

A too open sacral chakra can be characterized by a person being manipulative and hypersensitive.

A balanced, healthy sacral chakra results in a person having a healthy emotional behavior as well as confident artistic abilities.

ChakraCize: Sacral Chakra ~ Hula Hoop

The hula hoop is not only fun but loosens your lower back, which opens energy flow to your waistline. Do not worry if you do not have a hula hoop, this chakracize can be done with or without a hula hoop; you just have to move your hips!

Step 1: Stand up and make sure you have enough room around you. Extend your arms out to the sides.

Step 2: Start moving your hips in a circular shape from left to right or right to left.

Affirmation: "I accept my reality as I have created."

Solar Plexus

The solar plexus chakra is your third chakra. It is located within your solar plexus area, above your bellybutton and below your ribcage. The solar plexus holds all your power and the energy that says "I AM".

When the solar plexus is blocked, you show insecurities and lack of self-confidence. You do not hold your power at all.

A too open solar plexus chakra carries judgmental and arrogant energy. The ego moves in and starts to take over all the power, leaving you posing as a person you are not.

With a balanced solar plexus, you are in control and holding you power. Your self-respect spills over into all aspects of your life.

ChakraCize: Solar Plexus ~ Dance

The chakracize for the solar plexus is to DANCE, DANCE like nobody is watching! Dancing is a great way to reconnect with the earth while increasing your oxygen flow throughout your body.

You do not have to be a professional dancer to do this chakracize. You can dance in your closet, anywhere! Dancing is guaranteed to boost your spirit.

Affirmation: "I honor myself and Hold MY power!"

Heart Chakra

The fourth chakra is your heart chakra. The heart chakra is your essence of joy, carrying all your universal love. When the heart chakra is blocked, you will experience a block of love. This includes a lack of love for yourself as well as others.

When your heart chakra is too open, you can be one who limits your love, offering conditional love to yourself and those in your life.

With a balanced heart chakra, you are able to love with pure intentions. There are no conditions or limits on giving and receiving love in your life.

ChakraCize: Heart Chakra ~ "Sending My Love"

This chakracize will encourage positive energy flow within your heart chakra—"Sending My Love". This chakracize will give you a sense of emotional empowerment while releasing emotional wounds that are stored in your heart chakra.

Step 1: Find a comfortable place to sit, one where you feel connected to self.

Step 2: Close your eyes and place your hands, one on top of the other, palms facing your chest, over your heart chakra.

Step 3: Visualize the most vibrant green light radiating within your heart chakra.

Step 4: Now take pieces of this green light and start sharing them with people that you love. Be generous and know that you have SO much love to give away, it will not ever run out.

Step 5: Be sure to give a piece of that love to yourself as well. Once you are done giving, take the time to appreciate being in the moment with so much love.

Affirmation: "I love myself and others unconditionally."

Throat Chakra

Your fifth chakra is your throat chakra. This chakra is located at the base of your throat and carries all communication energies. Throat chakras do not develop until we are about 8 years old; i.e. once we are old enough to know our truth.

The characteristics of a blocked throat chakra are lying and not speaking your truth.

When the throat chakra is too open, we can be overly talkative and self-centered.

A balanced throat chakra allows you to speak your truth; you are reliable and can communicate openly.

ChakraCize: Throat Chakra ~ Shoulder Stand

The chakracize for the throat chakra is the shoulder stand. This chakracize will release all constricted energy and allow positive energy to move into the upper chakras.

Step 1: Lie flat on your back, palms facing down.

Step 2: Lift your bottom and legs off the floor and point your feet toward the ceiling.

Step 3: Hold your lower body with your hands supporting your lower back off the floor. Stay in this position as long as you are comfortable.

Affirmation: "I always speak my truth!"

Third Eye (Brow) Chakra

Your sixth chakra is the third eye or brow chakra, located on your forehead between your eyebrows. Your third eye is your intuition energy. When it is blocked, the characteristics include being very distant from your gut feelings.

When the third eye chakra is too open, characteristics include being overly logical, analyzing all things.

A balanced third eye allows the being to draw on their intuitive powers and to know the unknowable, trusting their intuition in guiding their life.

The chakracize for the third eye is "Awakening My Intuition!" This chakracize will help ground you into the present moment and give you an overall sense of wellbeing.

ChakraCize: Third Eye/Brow Chakra ~ Awakening My Intuition

Step 1: Sit in a comfortable position.

Step 2: Place your hands, one on top of the other, palms down, placed over the heart chakra.

Step 3: Raise your hands with palms facing out, and place a hand on each side of the third eye chakra.

Step 4: Raise hands above your body and return hands to heart chakra. Repeat as many times as you would like.

Affirmation: "I trust my inner self."

Crown Chakra

Your chakra system ends with the crown chakra at the top of your head. This chakra carries the energy of your spirituality, you connection with source.

A blocked crown chakra results in lack of purpose and weak moral beliefs.

When a crown chakra is too open, a being can feel spiritually overloaded, questioning all spirituality.

A balanced crown chakra allows for a profound awakening or quantum moment, being so connected spiritually that you are at your integrated best.

ChakraCize: Crown Chakra ~ Headstand

The chakracize for the crown chakra is the headstand. This chakracize will align your spinal column while encouraging mental clarity.

Step 1: Get in headstand position—on all fours with palms flat.

Step 2: Lift your body up with feet toward the ceiling.

Affirmation: "I am one with Universal Love."

Masculine ~ having qualities appropriate to or usually associated with a man

Feminine ~ characteristic of or appropriate or unique to women

Energy ~ The power by which anything acts effectively

Honor all parts of your energetic makeup, both *your feminine and masculine energies; for these two energies make up the divine being you are. Celebrate your whole.*

One Being, Two Energies

We are all divine beings, holding both masculine and feminine energies in our spirit. We often find ourselves displaying learned behavior, not allowing the expression of both masculine and feminine, limiting ourselves with expectations of societal pressures to show only gender-specific energies. There seems to be no room for a balance until now. As we evolve and change the dynamics of societal normalcy, we are no longer working so hard to separate the two energies. People are awakening to their true selves, owning all energetic parts.

Reality is that both energies are a part of creating our strongest emotions, allowing us to be who we are. As we pull out of our ego-based thinking, balancing the energies allows for a healing of the whole. The balance depends solely on what your inner self has learned to become. As you travel through your life journey, experiencing lessons made for your soul's growth, how you react to each situation depends on the personal balance of masculine and feminine energies.

Examining the inner self, we are able to determine what energy is strong and which is weak, allowing us to take charge and bring an energetic balance of both the masculine and the feminine. Know that it is ok to be a male with a strong feminine energy as well as it is ok to be a female with strong masculine energy. Do not allow yourself to be limited or defined based on society's view of what your energy should be. Your energy is your choice! Honor the self always! Learning about your masculine and feminine energies will allow you to look within and explore which energy you are strong in, allowing you to make changes where you desire.

Masculine energy represents a place of strength and knowing who you are, focusing on the value that *you* place on your self and your life. Having a weak masculine energy, you are likely to doubt yourself. You may not try new things, leaving yourself no room for progress on your path.

A strong masculine energy allows your life to be ego-driven, always working to show off anything you have been doing to feel a sense of self-gratification; displaying aggressive behaviors out of arrogance.

A balanced masculine energy allows you to be in control of your life, accomplishing all that you set out for with self-confidence but not arrogance; holding your head high, with your presence demanding attention whether you are speaking or not. A balanced masculine energy allows room for your feminine energy to take the appropriate place in your life.

Feminine energy represents a place of wholeness, focusing on the value others have in your life.

If you have weak feminine energy, you may label others of low worth in your life. This will result in being closed off socially, developing a victim personality, finding blame for your life. The weak feminine energy is very easy to spot in others, but can be a challenge to see this within ourselves. If we see it in ourselves, we must be accountable; so it is easier to point out issues in others.

A person who is overcome with feminine energy may become a doormat for others. The value placed on others is so high that you may want to give and give without thinking of yourself.

A balanced feminine energy allows you to know the value of others, encouraging a giving nature from within. You have such a sense of inner peace that interfering with others is unnecessary unless you are asked. Then, you are anxious to help in all ways so that you can to make their life better without taking from your own.

Living with a balance of the two energies, you will treat others the same way you treat yourself—living the golden rule as your personal rule.

Exercise #6: Reshaping Feminine vs. Masculine

1. Determine which areas of feminine and masculine energies you are lacking. Defining which energy is stronger will give you a starting point to balance the two.

2. To strengthen your masculine energy, start a chart that documents big and small accomplishments that build your confidence. Use affirmations to encourage a balanced energy: "I honor my masculine energy. I see my progress allowing me inner strength."

3. To strengthen your feminine energy, focus on allowance. Allow others to walk their own path, experiencing individual lessons without your expectations.

Inspiration ~ The quality or state of being inspired

Always remember those that stood by your side and supported you as you worked toward your dreams.

Igniting Your Fire

Defining who you are as an individual in a world where everyone is working so hard to make us all the same can be quite the experience. Our power lies in the fact that people are only in your life if you invite them in. Determining who influences your life, whether it is positive or negative, is entirely up to you. You have complete control of who participates in your life. So if someone is not adding positivity to your direction, it is time to remove them from the roster.

In an ego-based society, such as ours, we find that most people are threatened by the success of others. They may feel left behind as your dreams become a reality. As you are stepping closer to living your purpose, there will always be critics—those that do not see your vision and are quick to tell you why. When you find yourself coming across a naysayer, it is important to keep yourself grounded; to know that even though everyone is not going to support and agree with what you are doing, you are following your path, an inner knowing that you have. It is not important to have the validation of others for you to accomplish your purpose. It is important to keep your direction and follow your dreams. The best thing you can do in these situations is to do the work and prove the critics wrong.

On the other, more positive hand, you come across those certain people that believe in you and the direction you are headed—a person that inspires your light, encouraging you to get out there and accomplish all that you are. These are the people that you want to surround yourself with, those that appreciate and support who you truly are. The spiritual inspiration is amazing! I want you to know that you will do great things. I believe in you!

Those that light your inner flame, and want to see you succeed in all that you do, remind you of how powerful you are on this journey.

The way to weed out those that encourage you and those that discourage you is to be very picky about who you allow as a constant in your life.

Know that people that do not believe in you do not need to be a part of your life. Their negativity is a lack of confidence within themselves; so they are unable to share positivity with you. Do not make their mindset your business—it is not yours; it is never yours. Allow yourself the space to create and accomplish your purpose. It is not about building walls against others; it is about honoring yourself enough to not allow anyone to bring you down. Respect and honor your endeavors enough to remove those that do not support you. This is not about them; this is about you living your purpose.

Shine on!

I have experienced many people in my life that choose to live with negativity toward my work. They are quick to belittle me and try to take away what I stand for. I know they have lived in a pattern of unhappiness for so long that they do not realize the results their actions have on others. The ego has them living an illusion that judging and belittling others will make them superior. Seeing themselves so separate from the whole, they are unable to see the reality that there is an abundance of everything for everyone! Abundance does not run out; there is plenty for everyone.

As these people present themselves into my reality, I take the time to be kind but aware of their negative behaviors. I choose to surround myself with those that believe in me and want to see me succeed, always knowing that it is my responsibility to choose those that surround me.

Exercise #7: Reshaping Your Surroundings

1. Realize that each person in your life is invited in by you. You allow all the negativity and positivity each person brings into your life.

2. When you find those that believe in you, appreciate them, support them, and stick close to them.

3. Weed out the individuals that have nothing nice to say to you. It is not important to have people in your lives that do not know you are wonderful.

Creating ~ To bring into existence

*Every success has started as one person's idea. They took the idea,
Believed that it would work, Created it, and MADE it happen!
We each have this opportunity.*

Today, chase your dreams and make them happen.

You... The Creator

Can you see your future? Your name in lights, people waiting in lines to see you, writing that best seller? We all have dreams, aspirations, and goals that we can envision within our minds. Each time you have these visions, you move one step closer to accomplishing your dreams. You are able to start directing energy toward these goals by your thought patterns. Since you are the sole creator in your life, the power is in your hands. You can sit around and wonder and wait for life to bring you what you want or you can get up and get going creating it! You must be willing to do the work to turn these dreams into reality. Three easy steps for creating are: envision it happening; work at making it happen; and believe it will happen!

So much of life is spent sitting around waiting for the weather to be right, waiting for the perfect job, waiting for more money, etc. It is time to quit waiting and start doing! There is no cap on the abundance available within the universe. Abundance is ever flowing; all you have to do is be open to receiving it. It's easy to think some people have all the luck; nothing could be further from the truth. The difference between people experiencing absolute abundance and those that do not is the desire to make it happen.

We spend so much of our time talking and talking instead of doing. It is time to take a hands-on approach to our lives, progressing on our journey, and creating reality from our dreams.

A great way to start making stuff happen in your life is with creative visualization exercises. Creative visualization allows you to be in the space where energy is created; you start building a strong energetic vibe to send out to the universe. This encourages the energy to get flowing to bring you everything that you want. Welcome it, accept it, and enjoy it. Abundance is yours!

Let's try a creative visualization: Take three deep breaths to center; start to visualize what you desire, whether it is a job, a spouse, a new car—whatever you want. Do not allow any mind chatter only focus on what you want to create for yourself. Hold the image for five minutes, allowing yourself to see, feel, hear, smell and touch all that your vision has to offer. This will start the energy flowing toward creating your dreams. Know that you deserve all that you desire and that you are worth creating this into your life. Practice as often as needed.

When I find myself in situations where I want something, I become consumed with making it happen. I don't want to just talk about it; I want to get up and make it happen! When I decided to write my first book *Awakening Consciousness: A Girl's Guide*, I was in that mindset. I had spent months looking for a book that would encourage awareness while enhancing self-esteem for my four girls whom I was homeschooling. I bought many books online and visited bookstores only to be disappointed. All the books I found were telling me what to do but were not giving the girls any hands-on activities that would encourage them. After three months of searching and practicing my creative visualizations, I turned to my girls and said "that's it! I am writing it." A spiritual inspiration came over me and I was moving forward, no matter what. Limits did not even enter my mind because I was making it happen. I contacted Loving Healing Press, and the rest is history. Not once did I question that I was meant to write it; it came so easily and has helped so many.

So there you go friends; once you stop talking and start doing, life will flow smoothly, opening all doors just for you! When you mix your passion with your purpose, the possibilities are endless! Let's get started!

Exercise #8: Reshaping Your Future

1. **Start a Vision Board or Quote Board.** These are simple ways to remind you of what you are working toward. Use old magazines and cut out pictures of your dreams, or write quotes that motivate you and hang them around your house, somewhere that you see it all the time.

2. **Practice creative visualization activities.** The more you visualize yourself with your dreams accomplished, the more energy you are sending out to create.

3. **Stop talking and start doing.** No more excuses and no more waiting. It is in your hands.

Judging ~ To hold as an opinion: guess, think

Do not be so quick to judge others. Judging others does not define them. It defines you.

Open your eyes and mind to seeing love, beauty, and kindness in each person.

Remember that we are all sharing the path

Mirror, Mirror on the Wall

We live our lives through the perception we have of ourselves, of others, and of life in general. Life is how we see it. Everything, and I mean everything, is only as you see it. We base each choice we make, each judgment we have, completely on our perceptions. The good news is that there is plenty of time to open our eyes wider and see things from a different perspective, allowing you to reshape your reality.

As we live, we develop an idea of who we are and who we are supposed to be. This is our self-perception. Self-perception is all about how we see ourselves, what we look in the mirror and think about ourselves. We develop these self-perceptions as we grow. Each of us is labeled by our parents, teachers, clergy, society... and the list goes on and on. Until we are old enough to evaluate what parts of our self-image are ours and what parts have been learned behavior, we remain the same. It is time to free yourself from imposed labels and start defining yourself from your authenticity. Our entire life is based off who we think we are; it determines each step of our life. If you perceive yourself as a confident, powerful person, you are likely to get out there and live with zest, having no limits accomplishing your goals, always moving forward, believing in yourself. If you look at yourself as a person lacking confidence—not quite good enough, creating limits in what you can do—that is the life you will live. It is time to change any negative perception you have of yourself. It is important to know your divinity. Since it is up to you how you see yourself, then why not see your true self—the light that shines so bright. Why not accept that you are perfect just as you are.

Start today by looking in the mirror and affirming to yourself, "I am perfect NOW." Say it, repeat, and believe it. The more you repeat this, the sooner it becomes your truth. Perception is in the eye of the beholder. Remember that we all find ourselves judging others at times. This is not about defining someone else; it is solely about defining ourselves. We judge others based on our perceptions. Finding fault in others allows us to feel power, feel superior to them. This is ego, all ego. You start taking away from who they are because of the image you hold of yourself. Each person we encounter acts as a mirror, allowing us to see who we are, revealing our true issues and true inner state.

If you are quick to find anger in others, take a look at the anger within. If you see love in others, be assured this is a direct reflection of your love. You define yourself each time you make a judgment.

Instead of seeing the greatness in others, we find ourselves focusing on the negative aspects of who they are. We become frustrated because we are unable to make sense of what they are doing. We question their values, morals, and common sense, based on our morals, values, and common sense. In some situations, we find ourselves so obsessed with fixing what others are doing that it becomes a part of our identity. It sounds silly, but think of how many times you have stopped what you are doing to be overly consumed with what others are doing, saying, or not doing and not saying. We forget that each relationship we experience reflects a lesson our soul needs. As I encounter relationships with others that just get me frustrated, I have to remind myself that there is a lesson there. Each time I ask myself what do I need from this. In the past, I would find myself judging and badmouthing others that offended me because it made me feel better about myself. I would repeat the story over and over to others to justify myself and find others who would support what I had felt. I felt that need to demean others for personal satisfaction.

As I have grown, learned about myself and gained confidence, I am able to look for the divinity in others—releasing myself from fixing them, allowing myself to seek out my lesson, accept it, and move forward. By living with an open mind, we are able to invite the lesson and see what this person brings to the table for our lesson. Face it, we are not going to agree with the behavior others choose; but being able to look past that and allow them to be who they are will free us. We will start to seek out the divinity and love that run through everyone, leaving judgment by the wayside. Always seek out the light of others; it will only add to your shine!

Exercise #9: Reshaping Your Judgment

1. Use a rubber band on your wrist; each time you pass a judgment, snap it, reminding you that judging is not the way to go

2. See past the lack of knowing in others and open your eyes to seeing divine love flowing in each person.

3. Create an affirmation, each time you judge others, about liking yourself. Eventually, it will become a truth for you and a habit. You will no longer need to judge others.

Kindness ~ The quality of being kind; good will; a kind act

Be the hand that catches the fall of others,
encouraging, uplifting, and uniting as one
hand in hand, building humanity.

Because Nice Matters

Nice matters; it always matters. The world you are living in, breathing in, is the world you have created. Each moment, we have the choice to live with kindness. Whatever you are living your life with will reflect in all you do. It has been proven in many studies that those committing an act of kindness increase their happiness levels as well those that are receiving the act of kindness. Do we really need a study to tell us that? One act of kindness will ripple out into the world and change the entire energy of the whole. It's simple as this... just be nice!

We often find being kind to others is easy. It is being kind to ourselves where we struggle. Do you remember the last time you told yourself "good job"? It is typical to be hard on ourselves because we are the biggest critic of ourselves. We find fault in many things we do because of our ego beliefs—of having to be the best. There is no patience for growth or mistakes because they are ours and we must not falter. Next time you are giving yourself a hard time, step back and look at yourself as if you were your friend or a child. As you start to belittle and criticize yourself, think of how you would treat the friend or child in the same situation. You would never be so harsh to a friend or child who is learning and growing; so why are you so mean to you? You would be supportive, sharing confidence for them. Today, you do this for yourself, showing yourself the kindness you deserve. You are constantly learning and growing; allow yourself that.

Think back to the people in your life that stand out. Who are they? I bet they are the people who treated you with kindness and love. Those moments that we write home about are those we attach "feel-good" emotions to, because in those moments, we experienced some form of kindness. Be the person that people remember by being kind to everyone and everything. Kindness is so easy; try it, you'll see.

It is so fantastic when we meet certain people in life who have an everlasting effect on who we are as a person. It is their kindness that we remember, the emotions we attached to that moment. The first person that I remember being kind to me was my kindergarten teacher, Mrs. Castaneda. It was such a relief to escape the realities of the abusive home life and be in a classroom that was full of love and kindness. She never judged me because of the lifestyle I lived or that my parents were drug abusers; she only showed unconditional love and kindness. I often think of her and the impact a person can have on you. This motivates me to be kind to all whom I meet. It reminds me that in life we remember those who are kind, not those with the biggest bank accounts or the fanciest cars. It is the profound moment that someone touches the depth of your spirit with kindness that your life shifts. It is the burst of life force you feel as when you are touched by the kindness of others.

It is always an option to be nice. We find so many people who build up walls because they have been taught to not let others in, not to be kind because the world is full of mean people. This is a lie. If you are seeing the world full of hateful, unkind individuals, then it is what you will live. That is what you will invite into your daily living. It is important to be nice, even if others are not always nice to you. We are nice because that is the kind of person we are, not because we gain brownie points from others; because nice matters, all day, every day!

Exercise #10: Reshaping Kindness

1. **Practice random acts of kindness:** open a door for a stranger; let someone in while you are driving; pay for the coffee of someone behind you; and the list goes on and on

2. **Share a smile.**

3. **Send an old-fashioned handwritten letter** to an old friend, telling them how great they are and how you appreciate them.

Right ~ The correct or factual report or interpretation of something

Wrong ~ In a wrong direction, place or manner; erroneously

It's not about being right or wrong. It is about living your truth while allowing others to live theirs.

Today, set aside your need to be right, when it comes to the lives of others, and focus on your own life.

It is not up to you to determine what is right and wrong for others; it is up to you to determine what is right or wrong for you.

I'm Right, You're Wrong.... You're Right, I'm Wrong

What if I told you that you are always right and I am always right? It would be the truth. We are each right because we each see our lives through individual perceptions. Like I mentioned earlier, personal perception determines everything.

All battles start with the "I'm right, you're wrong" issue, a power struggle to show dominance. In most situations, each person has predetermined their truth and will stick by it, no matter what. Why do we make this such a pertinent part of our lives? We explode with arrogance, knowing we are right, making us the power player in the disagreement. We stand with our chest out, king of the mountain! It seems like we have been programmed that if we are found to be wrong, we are weak—a disillusion that we will lose part of who we are if we are found to be wrong. We will walk to the ends of the earth, end marriages, give up friendships, lose jobs—all to exhibit how right we are; sacrifice all happiness just to look at the other person in the eyes and say, "Ha, I told you so. I was right!"

Who are we to decide what is right and what is wrong? Is there even such a thing as right and wrong? If so, who decides the guidelines for these situations? The truth of the matter is that being right and being wrong is subjective. It is not important.

What is important is knowing and allowing that we each have our own views, our own opinions; staying true to your convictions while allowing others to have their convictions without labels and judgment of right versus wrong. Accepting into your reality that every person you encounter is right in their own truth will allow you to relax and let others live their own path. You can quit spending so much time trying to convince others you are right and get more time living your passions. I often hear people arguing over who is right and who is wrong. I watch parents pointing fingers at their children, spouses declaring rightness against each other, patrons arguing with clerks at stores, belligerently demanding they know what's right. It is an unending battle *of I know more than you do.*

It is time that we allow everyone to see things in their way and it is not our job to tell them they are right or wrong. Imagine the peace that would ripple throughout our world if we just allowed everyone the courtesy of being right, letting each individual live their truth while we live ours.

Next time you find yourself in a disagreement, just look the person in the eye and say, "I see your viewpoint and although it differs from mine, I accept it." And move on in your life.

I have found myself consumed with proving I am right in how a family member chooses to live her life. I disagree with pretty much her whole life. I spent countless days arguing on the phone with her about what she should be doing and what she shouldn't be doing and how I had her life all figured out for her. As I came to the realization that I just may not know what is right for her, I made a face-to-face apology, and I told her that I might not agree with her lifestyle but I was letting it go. I will no longer fight over who is right and who is wrong. She is right in her eyes and I am right in mine. Live and let live. Allow yourself the knowing that we can all be right all the time. It is knowing this fact whereby you are able to release yourself from the burden of always being right. Just accept, allow, and let be.

Exercise #11: Reshaping Right Vs. Wrong

1. Realize that we all are entitled to our opinions, and that's all that they are—individual opinions. They are not right or wrong, just different. Honor your opinions while allowing others to honor theirs.

2. Stop yourself in an argument of who's right or wrong, and just BE. Be confident that being in peace is more important than being right or wrong.

3. Don't take a right-or-wrong stance on issues. Just allow whatever is to be.

Happiness ~ Enjoying, giving or indicating pleasure; being joyous

Happiness starts with self, ends with self, and is all about SELF.

Happiness is a Choice, Your Choice!

Are you happy? What if I told you, you could be perfectly happy right now, in this moment? Well, guess what, that is what I am telling you! Happiness is not in what you do but how you do in life. It becomes a personal choice each moment of your life. In life, we find happiness with our families, with our careers, with our hobbies, but forget to find the happiness within. We spend so much time searching for happiness from outside sources, forgetting we hold the key within ourselves.

The happiness of self must become a priority. We cannot give what we do not have. It is not possible for you to share your happiness with the world if you cannot find it yourself. Happiness lies within. Although material things, possessions, and relationships bring joy, they do not supply the true happiness so many long to have.

Happiness is this feeling of peace, a sense of contentment—the amazing feeling of completion as you look at your life, living complete and whole without limitations. The fantastic thing about happiness is that it is 100% self-created. You hold all the power when it comes to this. The sooner you realize that happiness is your personal responsibility, the sooner you will quit looking to outside sources. This only limits and removes happiness from who you are as a whole. Past beliefs have us limited to thinking that if we are invested in our own happiness, we are selfish. Taking the time to care for yourself is not being selfish at all; it is critical to your health. It is time to defeat the myth that we must have that perfect spouse, best friend, etc, in order to find happiness. So much of our lives is spent looking for that special someone that is going to make life worth living.

The fact of the matter is you attract what you are; so if you are so consumed with finding someone to make you happy instead of living happiness within, you are missing the target altogether. It is unfair to put the responsibility of your happiness on someone else. Your emotions are yours; stand up and take responsibility for them. As you become happy from within, you will attract that special someone to share your happiness.

Do not ever depend on others to make you happy. Always hold your happiness in your hands; that way, it's never out of reach.

When I first started out on my personal journey, the first book I read was about personal happiness. I was amazed. It had never occurred to me that I could be in charge of my own happiness. I was always looking for someone or something to bring joy to my life. Wow! What a burden I was putting on others, leaving it up to them to make me happy! As I discovered my happiness was my choice, I began to see life differently. I noticed that my emotions were controlled by me. If I wanted to be happy, that was it; I could be happy without my mom saying I could, without my husband saying I could. I no longer would allow the behaviors or emotions of others determine my mood. Now I wake up each day knowing that if I want to be happy today, it is my choice, no matter what comes my way during the day.

Today, you become invested in your personal happiness. Search your inner self and discover what makes you happy. Quit waiting for others to allow your happiness. It is yours and it is time to own it!

Exercise #12: Reshaping Personal Happiness

1. Explore what makes you happy. Find your individual pleasures that define your personal happiness.

2. Make a commitment to do something for personal happiness once a week. This can only be for you!

3. Take 5 minutes a day for self, enjoying *you*.

Love ~ A very great interest or fondness;
to take pleasure or delight in; like very much

Love yourself... That's it. Simple. Let's start today.

Love Yourself... Simple

Love yourself; love others; love the world! Love is a word that cannot be used enough. Love is defined as a very great interest or fondness to take pleasure or delight in; to like very much. How do you define love? I define love as an unconditional feeling of bliss, being so overwhelmed with the moment that you lose track of time and reality. The intensity of love is fantastic! There is nothing stronger than the feeling of love; it heals everything. Love for yourself will move mountains and change your entire outlook on life.

There is so much pressure put on the words "I love you." We are taught to attach such an intense emotion to the word. This adds expectations to those you say it to and to those that say it to you. It is time to remove the pressure and just allow "I love you" to heal yourself and the world.

As we grow up, we are taught that love should be hoarded and only shared with those that are most deserving in exclusive situations. We might say "I love you" to our parents, our siblings; but to tell a friend that you love them is not allowed and makes some people uncomfortable. I disagree with this; we need to remove this thinking pattern and see we are all love—that love runs very strong through each of us. Love is so big, it never runs out and should be given away by bucketfuls!

While you are busy giving away all this love, you must remember the most important person who needs your love is YOU! As we love ourselves, we gain confidence and start to perceive life with a new outlook. We are able to remove limitations we have created for ourselves, allowing an unconditional love to flow from ourselves, within ourselves and to others. If we are lacking self-love, we find ourselves pining for attention from anyone who will give it.

We start to believe we deserve nothing because we do not feel worthy of love. The lack of self-love leaves us feeling like our life is not worth anything. This is a problem for many people who find themselves trapped in poor relationships, allowing themselves to be abused emotionally, mentally, and sometimes physically. Although the relationship is dysfunctional and sometimes dangerous, the need to be needed outweighs the value we have for ourselves. Once we are able to own our self-love, the stronger our confidence gets and we begin to demand respect from others.

It is time for you to start loving yourself. Start today to work on your self-value by standing in the mirror, looking in your eyes, and saying, "I Love You". As you do this, listen to the mind chatter that comes up. This chatter will allow you to see where you need to start healing. Then write affirmations for each part of you that you are not loving and hang them on your mirror. Read them, repeat them, breathe them! Own your worth!

I have watched my mom, from as far back as I can remember, struggle with loving herself. She is constantly looking at herself and doubting her worth. This contributed to my belief of what I was worth as I was growing up. My mom displayed no self-worth and she attracted abusive men, allowing them to abuse her. Her lack of self-love left her open to the attitude of "better to be abused than to be alone". As a child, we are constantly learning who we are, defining ourselves by the people that are influencing our lives. It is an unsettling effect the people you live with as a child have on you as you grow up.

I suffered from low self-esteem for the better part of my life. As a teenager, I turned to alcohol and boys to supplement the attention I felt was lacking in my life. I made all my choices based on my belief of what I was worth, and that was very little. Becoming a mother at age 17 was a wakeup call like no other. As I was told that I was having a little girl, I made the commitment to raise my daughter with self-esteem, self-love, and confidence. This is when I decided to change because I knew my self-worth would directly affect her.

I had to look at my life and really decide how I would reprogram myself with self-confidence. I realized that I had been giving away so much of my power trying to find someone to validate me, to tell me I was good enough. It was an amazing time in my life when I determined that I was the one that had to decide I was good enough. So I started making choices to honor myself, I stopped looking for outside attention and started finding my peace inside. It is a miraculous feeling when you find your power.

I made the choice to live fully, being an example for my daughter by looking myself in the mirror and telling myself "I love you", and meaning it. It transformed my entire life as I gained a sense of worth for myself, no longer allowing myself or anyone else to abuse me. It is a freedom that allows you to own your power and live a life of love, sharing the love you have for yourself with all that touch your life. Yes friends, self-love is that powerful.

Exercise #13: Reshaping Love

1. Each day, look in the mirror and say "I love you just as you are." Do this at least 3 times or until you don't feel self-conscious or embarrassed about doing it.

2. Make a list of reasons why you love yourself. Hang it in a place you will find yourself looking at it often.

3. Be an example for others. You cannot just talk about self-love; you must live that self love! Give love to everyone and everything you see.

Gratitude ~ A feeling of thankfulness

It is such a privilege to be alive. Don't waste your time complaining about what you don't have or don't like in your life. Just live each moment.

Celebrate Life.

Raise Your Glass

There is confusion throughout humanity that life owes us something. In the great scheme of things, we feel that we are a gift to life when in reality, life is a gift to us; it is just being awake enough to see it. We find things to complain about, like the sun being too hot, the snow being too cold, the wind messing up our hair. I don't know about you, but complaining about all that small stuff seems ridiculous. Life is a privilege; do not play small with it. Just the fact that you get to be a part of this world is a chance to make the world a better place. Opportunity surrounds you; it is just being aware of it. It is up to you how you take the opportunities of life and run with them.

If you are looking for a way to start enjoying your life, gratitude is the place to start. Living in a state of gratitude will shift the entire way you are living. It's about finding appreciation for all areas of life, even the bumps and bruises, and using them to propel you into a life of purpose. You must look within and discover what matters and what doesn't. Remove your focus from the small stuff that really doesn't matter and focus on the *realness* of life— those things that make it worth it, like your children laughing, feeling good inside, breathing, the things that are irreplaceable.

Are you seeing life with your rose-colored glasses? Try accepting, appreciating the opportunities of seeing sunshine, feeling the grass between your toes, just being alive!

A sense of gratitude comes from within, a mindful choice. It is a conscious act made by you to start living, creating and attracting gratitude into your daily living. As soon as you find gratitude in anything big or small, you shift your mindset into a state of positivity.

We all have our days. Some mornings, we wake up on the wrong side of the bed, leaving us in a bad mood. This is when it becomes imperative that we take charge of our day. I can always find things to be grateful for shifting my mood. And you can too! It can be something as simple as your favorite cereal in the cupboard. Try this little activity the next time you are feeling down and I promise you that you can change your mood. Look around your house and find something simple as a plant that brings you joy. As you find the gratitude in having this plant, you will instantly raise your vibrations and shift your mood. This may take a few tries, but you will get it. So keep at it! You cannot stay in a state of despair and a state of gratitude at the same time. Choose gratitude!

In my past I would find myself focusing on what wasn't in my life instead of all that was there. It is easy to see what is missing when that is what you are looking for. By slowing down and opening my heart and mind to all that I have to be grateful for has allowed me to live a life of gratitude—shifting my entire life. Now when I look around at the trees, the river, my family, my home, my life I am able to really experience the greatness I am surrounded by and live with gratitude.

It is really a personal choice. I choose to live optimistic because I know this life is a privilege that so many do not get. I also know that 100 years goes real fast, especially if you are not living each day to its fullest. If I wake up with negativity, I am quick to change my state of mind by listing all the things I am grateful for, including being able to see, to eat, to breathe and it shifts me instantly. I won't waste one second of this life. Since this is my life, my choice, it is going to be damn good! Today, choose to live life with gratitude, appreciating all that you have created and all that you are creating each moment.

Exercise #14: Reshaping Gratitude

1. Start a gratitude journal, listing all the small things you are thankful for.

2. Create an instant gratification list, writing 15 things that instantly brings a smile to your face.

3. Explore your house, finding all things that you are grateful for—your favorite foods, a beautiful houseplant, etc. Make a mental note of these and when vibrations are low, come back to them and shift yourself into gratitude!

Past ~ Having existed or taken place in a period before the present

Do not allow others to make you feel bad about the choices you have made in your life; past or present. Your feelings belong to you.

Choose to feel good—in this moment, in the next moment, in every moment.

If Only I Could've, I Should've, I Would've...

There is an epidemic taking over our world! It's a condition running rampant that we all have or had at one time. It is the IOC or the "If Only Condition". It is a mental chatter that consumes a majority of our lives. Stop and think of how many times you have said I could've, should've, boy I would've today or in the last week? If this sounds like you, you have caught the all-too-common "If Only Condition" or "IOC", polluting your mind with all sorts of could'ves, should'ves and would'ves that are limiting your life. We find ourselves using these *If Onlys* because it buys us more time for whatever choices we have or haven't made. It allows us to create an excuse for why life is where it is; why we never finished that project; what we could have done to change that—all excuses to stall personal responsibility.

Life is very real and we all make mistakes. We all want to change things we have done and haven't done in our journey. It is fine to see where we could have changed certain things, but the problem is that we continue on a walk of shame and blame our entire lives. Unable to move past what we could've, should've, would've because we must punish ourselves for the past *if onlys*. The IOC works by distorting your now moments and creating blame, guilt, and self-doubt for what could have been. As an adult, we see life full of moments where we could sit back and use the "if only condition" to blame ourselves for any shortcomings. In reality, life lives in the present moment only. You cannot "fix" what is already done.

Unless you have superpowers or a time machine to go back to the moment that you would change and grab something off the table, you cannot change the past. We must accept the choices of the past and move forward in the *now*, freeing ourselves from the feelings of inadequacy because we could've, should've, would've.

I too have found myself a product of the IOC, filling my mind with should'ves. I catch myself saying I should've done this; I should have done that. It becomes frustrating and overwhelming as I play with the illusion that "I should've" will fix what I did not do. As I catch myself in this behavior, I say out loud, "Stop! I accept responsibility for Now!" This always reminds me of the present moment and frees my mind of the *If Onlys!*

Exercise #15: Reshaping the "If Only Condition"

1. Stay in the present moment. As you start to fall victim to the "IOC", stop yourself by breathing deeply and try connecting with the present moment.

2. Forgive yourself for the past by losing the extra baggage. Face it people, you are not living in the past and you cannot change it, no matter how many times you feel guilt, blame yourselves, or doubt what you do now. *Now* is all that matters.

3. Replace "If only" with "I am", "I can", and "I do"—creating a connection to the *now* moment.

Unexpected ~ Not expected: unforeseen

It's exciting all the things we can do in this life, in this world. It is so limitless.

Expect nothing, Create everything!

Don't Expect That

If there is one thing that life will teach you over and over, it is to expect the unexpected. It is inevitable that change will present itself at each chance it gets, reminding you that the universe is in control. You will be headed in a direction with gusto, and BAM... life changes your course. This creates fear in us because we tend to fear change. It can leave us stagnant where we are, afraid to move forward. This fear must be faced so we can carry on with our lives. Be prepared, life is full of twists and turns that will surprise you in many ways; you will change directions a million times but in all of this, you will be moving toward your purpose—a purpose you have written into your blueprint of life. In those moments that you feel lost, when life is challenging you and to give up would be the easiest thing to do, these are the moments where the most change is taking place. You are growing and expanding toward the ultimate goal of your journey.

Use new circumstances to bounce to the next chapter of your life, accepting and learning all that you can. You can be shaken by the unexpected, but never defeated. If you lose your job, see it as an opportunity to move toward something you have always wanted to do, like go back to school, or start your own business—an open door to follow your passions. Pull the positive out. Accept that life flows as a river, always bending through the twists and turns, but always changing—always flowing past any blockages.

Life works on its own time, a divine timing where there are no *pause*, *rewind*, or *fast-forward* buttons for you.

All you encounter during this lifetime, and all those that follow, is happening exactly the way it was planned. Always work toward your goals and dreams but relax, knowing it will come in time. Just like you cannot stop the earth from turning, you cannot stop the divine flow of life. Acceptance frees you from expectations and is of utmost importance in this life.

This becomes so clear as you start to see your dreams becoming your reality! As we sit back and look at life, and where we started to where we are now, we can see just where life was flowing without any help from us. Take the time to think of where you were two years ago; what you were working for then; what goals you had; now look at where you are now—take notice in the progress you have made to your present moment. Pinpoint what actions you took in what areas of your life that led you right here. Then it all starts to make sense. You become confident as you start to expect the unexpected.

Each step taken, even if you didn't know it then, was leading to now. It comes together just as a puzzle comes together, piece by piece. Be proud of where you are and always honor the steps you have taken and are taking toward you purpose.

When I get discouraged, feeling like I am not progressing at the rate I want to be, I remind myself of divine timing. I look at where I was two years ago and the unopened box of dreams I had under my bed that I was talking about and not doing, and then I look at where I am now and realize that life is happening. I must allow myself the knowing that life will play out and I must step aside and let it! I am always working toward my goals, but I always have the knowing that all that I want is on its way!

Exercise #16: Reshaping the Unexpected

1. **Welcome change** into your life as it comes. Focus on the positive you can gain from each change.

2. **Go with the Flow.** Do not fight the divine timing of life. Just allow yourself to become like a river flowing peacefully toward your desired life.

3. **Do not be defeated by the unexpected.** Use these circumstances to open up a new chapter in your journey.

Coincidence ~ A remarkable occurrence of events, ideas, etc, at the same time or in the same way

Do not be afraid of what you never have seen or done.
Be excited to discover new abilities that will enhance your journey.

Hello, It's Me, *The Universe*

Does coincidence exist, or is it all a message being given by the ultimate, our universe or higher power? How often do you find yourself thinking of someone and then they call, or you run into each other in the grocery store? Do you catch yourself saying, "I was just thinking of you?"; finding yourself coming up on an accident that you missed by two minutes because you had to run back into your house for something. Are you a believer in coincidence? Do you see things happening with precision, or is life more of a free-for-all? I am confident that coincidences are requested by each individual experiencing them. They present themselves into our lives at just the right moment to share a lesson. Since we have determined that we are the creators of our lives, in charge of this magnificent journey, we must also be in charge of this part too. In this life, we are students participating in lessons that will benefit the soul— situations that create a healing for us to move forward. Coincidences are nothing more than self-reminders of what we are here to do—wake up notices to keep us on track, like an alarm clock that keeps going off even when we hit snooze; it continues to alert us. These little reminders will continue to present themselves as coincidences until we start to get it. For example, how the perfect teacher appears out of the blue with the lesson we are looking for; the ideal song comes on for the state of mind we are in that moment; we pick up a book and open right to the page we need to read for a message we need that day. These are requested soul messages to encourage us. These are times of serious growth and it may take a lifetime to see them as that; but the sooner we are able to find the lesson, the sooner our mind and hearts can heal.

A great way to prove that coincidences are requested by you in your life is to practice *mindful coincidences*. You can do this by thinking of a certain person that you may not see often. Have a clear image of this person and telepathically invite them frequently into your life. Watch as they start to appear, maybe through a phone call or a mention in a conversation. This will strengthen your belief in creating.

We are the sole creators of this life and when open to our powers, we are limitless. As you come across a coincidence in your life, be open to receiving the messages the universe is sending your way. Pay attention and take what you need to move forward on this glorious journey of life.

Exercise #17: Reshaping Your Message

1. **Pay attention** to all coincidences and accidents that present into your life. Try to see the message being sent by opening your heart and mind.

2. **Create coincidences** within your life with visualization activities, seeking out the reminders that come with each coincidence you face.

3. **Act on wake-up calls.** These are messages directed to you. Do not ignore them; otherwise, they will keep coming.

Release ~ To relieve from something that confines, burdens, or oppresses

Do not allow others to talk you down.
There are always those other people who are threatened by your shine.
Shine anyways!

Stand confident, loving who you choose to be in this life.

Let that Go

Today is the perfect day to let it go... let all the hurt, anger, and frustration go. Throughout our lives, people have wronged us, hurt our feelings, and just been rude. Unfortunately, these parts of our lives become the hardest to let go of. We fester in the plan for revenge, self-pity, and negativity. We choose to internalize the way we are treated by others, giving them so much power over our emotional state and allowing their negative actions to define who we are. I always remember my aunt saying to family members, when they were upset and out of sorts, "It's their stuff; why are you taking it on? It's not yours." Although I was hearing it, I was not really sure what to do with it. I mean shouldn't I care what others have to say about me, and why should anyone get away with treating me bad? It's up to me to make them pay for what they did. As I became a conscious adult, I was able to put her advice to use in my life. By not taking on the stuff of others, you are able to keep your inner peace without losing any integrity. You can allow them to be who they are with no disturbance of who you are. It does not mean the other person is getting away with anything; it means we are not allowing them to own your emotions. Taking on the stuff of others is a for-sure way to limit yourself and give away your power. You must start to see that we cannot control how others think of us or how they choose to react to who we are. The only thing we can control is how much of their emotions we take on. What parts of them we allow into our lives. Carrying around other people's stuff is solely your choice. So choose wisely what you hold onto and let the rest go!

You can invite in the drama and bad feelings associated with being treated badly, or you can know that it is none of your business what others think or say about you. Do not become so consumed in the drama of other lives that you begin to attract the drama to your own life. Each time we harbor anger for these people, we are allowing them to have power over us. We find ourselves wrapped up in hating, holding grudges, gossiping, and bringing ourselves down to a negative level, losing part of who we are. The choice they make to live negatively is their choice; how we react is ours. It is time to rise up and forgive these people and move forward on a positive path. You are taking charge of your power by not allowing anyone to hold your emotions hostage.

Back in the day, I was consumed by the emotions of others. I could not handle the thought of someone talking about me and not liking me. It would haunt me. I would lose an entire day after hearing gossip traveling through the family about me. As I became confident in myself, I was able to determine that I put way too much responsibility on others for my emotional state. It is all about letting others control my state of mind. I needed to let go—let go of trying to control the thoughts and opinions of others. What anyone thinks of me is none of my business. As I made a conscious decision in my life to let go and let live, I no longer take on other people's stuff. If others gossip about me, it is fine because then I know they are leaving everyone else alone! Accepting that how I feel is within me allows what others feel to be theirs. It is not up to anyone how I feel; it is only up to me. Live and let live!

Exercise #18: Reshaping "Letting It Go"

1. Do not repeat the story over and over to everyone you know. This leaves you reliving the negative situation, and the more you relive it, the more energy is put into it.

2. Write a letter to the person who wronged you. Explain how and why you were hurt. Then BURN IT!

3. Each time you think of the person that wronged you, send them love; they obviously need it.

Empower ~ To enable or permit

*Make a commitment with yourself today to live with positivity,
honoring who you are, living with confidence and self-love.
Accept that you are perfect and have nothing to prove.*

You're So Vain

I apologize to you if you have been misled to believe that you should hide your confidence—that being bold, knowing who you are, standing up for what you believe in makes you self-centered or conceited. Those that tell you this are mistaken. They have been taught a myth in life that they are not enough; that what they have to offer the world is of minimal importance. This is the number one issue we all face, not knowing we are enough. The programming starts in childhood and continues until we become confident within, knowing we are enough. The myth that we are not being enough for our parents, our teachers, our significant others makes us doubt if we are good enough for ourselves. We constantly try to outdo ourselves, so that others will tell us we are good enough. How silly does that sound that we need someone else to say, "Yep you are enough; you are awesome!" Is it so far off for us to just know this about ourselves? Can you look in the mirror with acceptance?

Today, try this exercise. Stop and ask yourself: *Am I good enough?* If you hesitate or answer with a "no", it is time to start healing within and move toward unconditional self-acceptance. You are a magnificent, complete person, holding all the tools needed to live a life of confidence. It is time to stop limiting yourself with these self-created beliefs and replace them with beliefs of strength, love, and personal validation. Stop allowing past programming to dictate how you feel in your life now. So what if your parents never said "good job!"; no one told you that you were beautiful; you never had money, *blah blah blah*; does it matter now? Only if you say it does.

If you are never confident in knowing that you are enough just as you are, you will continue to look for something your entire life that is already there. It is your decision now to have confidence. Remove the illusion—all that we are looking for is already right here, within each of us. I am telling you right now that you are enough. You must believe this within. The only validation you ever need is you own. It is a personal responsibility. If you are not seeing yourself with this image, it is time for change. *I AM ENOUGH!* Tape it to your mirror!

Exercise #19: Reshaping Your Confidence

1. **Love yourself.** It sounds simple, but is the hardest thing to accept. Stand in the mirror and say out loud "I love you!" while looking directly into your eyes. No negative chatter; only love for yourself.

2. **Stand strong** in your convictions. You know what is your truth your truth is and what has been programmed. Delete the programmed beliefs and stand in *your* truths.

3. **Be authentic** in all you do. Do not conform to fit in; it is never worth sacrificing who you are to be part of the crowd.

Journal

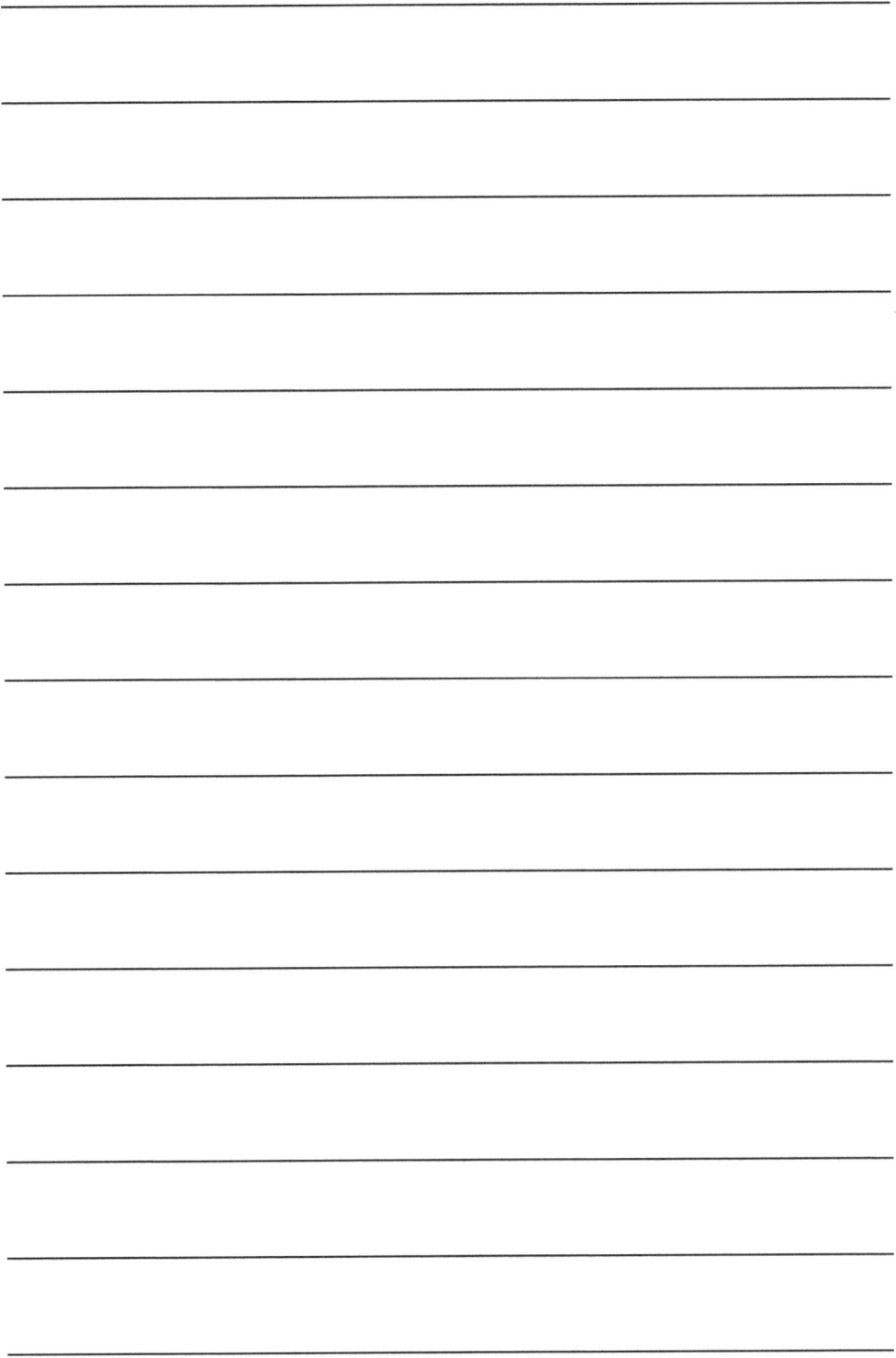

Epilogue

I am here to tell you, you are not a victim of your life. In your life, people will underestimate you, doubt you, criticize you—critics are everywhere. It makes no difference who has wronged you; how you were raised; what trauma you survived as a child. What matters is who you choose to be right now. This life is your privilege, so you better make it count. No more excuses, no more whining! From this point forward, you are the star player in your life! Do what you came here to do and do it with all you've got. I believe in you!

Love, Gratitude, and Kindness!
Robin Marvel

Bibliography

Brown, D. W. (2003). *Beginner's guide to crystals*. New York: Sterling Pub.

Dyer, W. (2001). *10 Secrets for Success and Inner Peace*. Carlsbad, CA :Hay House

Dyer, W. (2006). *Inspiration: Your Ultimate Calling*. Carlsbad, CA : Hay House

Lambert, M. (2005). *Natural highs for body & soul: Instant energizers to banish everyday energy lows*. London: Hamlyn. (Motivation, Self-Help)

MacLean, K. J. (2006). *The vibrational universe: Harnessing the power of thought to consciously create your life*. Potential of consciousness series, bk. 1. Ann Arbor, MI: Loving Healing Press. (motivational, self help)

Marvel, R. (2008). *Awakening Consciousness A Woman's Guide!"* Ann Arbor, Mi: Loving Healing Press.

Nacson, L. (1999). *Interpreting dreams A-Z*. Carlsbad, CA: Hay House.

Noyes, R. (2007). *The seven doors*. Gardners Books. (Metaphysical, non-fiction)

Paul, A. (2000). *Girlosophy: A soul survival kit*. Crows Nest, NSW: Allen & Unwin. (Children's Books, Self Help)

Petrinovich, T. S. (2002). *The call: Awakening the angelic human*. [United States]: Sar'h Pub. House. (metaphysical, motivation)

Ruiz, Don Miguel (2011). *The Fifth Agreement: A Practical Self Guide to Self Mastery*. Amber-Allen Publishing(Toltec Wisdom)

Seuss. (1990). *Oh, the places you'll go!* New York: Random House. (Children's Book)

Shane, S. (2006). *Spiritually awake in the physical world*. [United States]: Liquid Light Center. (metaphysical, motivation)

Silverstein, S. (1964). *The giving tree*. New York: Harper & Row.

Stein, D. (1987). *The Woman's Book of Healing*. The Crossing Point: Berkeley, CA (self help)

Tolle, E. (2005). *A new earth: Awakening to your life's purpose*. New York, N.Y.: Dutton/Penguin Group. (self-help)

Vaishali. (2006). *You are what you love*. [S.l.]: Purple Haze Press.

Wing, D. L. (2010). *The nature of tarot*. Ann Arbor, MI.: Marvelous Spirit Press (Metaphysical, Self Help)

Wolfe, A. (2003) *In the shadow of the shaman: Connecting with self, nature & spirit*. St. Paul, MN : Llewellyn (Self Help)

About the Author

Robin Marvel is a multi-published author and nationwide motivational speaker in the field of self-development. She has taken the negative situations she was dealt throughout her life and turned them into motivation and purpose, getting audiences on their feet, participating in the empowerment of their lives. You can find her online at **www.robinmarvel.com**.

Index

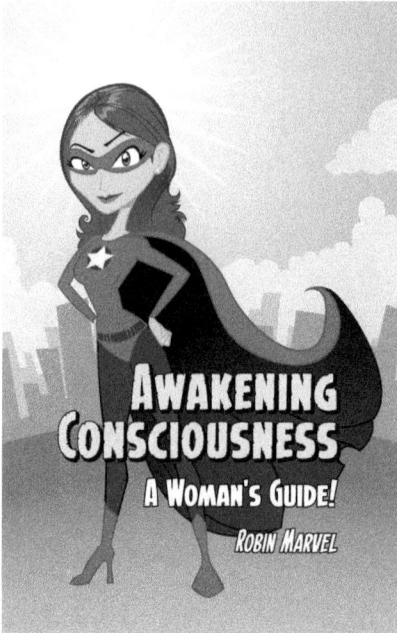

Are You Ready to Awaken the Power Within?

Be a woman of strength. Know you are an amazing, all creating individual. This guide will strengthen and encourage you to discover your inner core and create an empowered zest for life.

The exercises and crafts in this hands-on guide have been designed to Awaken your Consciousness on your path of self-awareness. You are on your way to ultimate love, tranquility and strength for your mind, body and soul. Grab your power, expand your awareness and never look back. Honor yourself by being true to who you are and sharing all that you are with the world.

Readers of this book will learn how to...

- ChakraCize Your Spirit
- Build Your Self Confidence
- Raise Your Vibrational Frequency with Ease
- Do Meditations to Create Your Life
- Discover Your Wisdom Within
- Care for Your Aura
- Unlock Your Dreams

"*Awakening Consciousness* encourages and guides the reader through fun exercises designed to get at the heart of spirituality and the practical application of that knowledge in their lives. Change does indeed begin from the bottom up!"

--Daniel Noyes, author *The Seven Doors*

ISBN-13: 978-1-61599-064-1
List Price: Paperback $ 17.95 / eBook $ 5.95

www.MarvelousSpirit.com

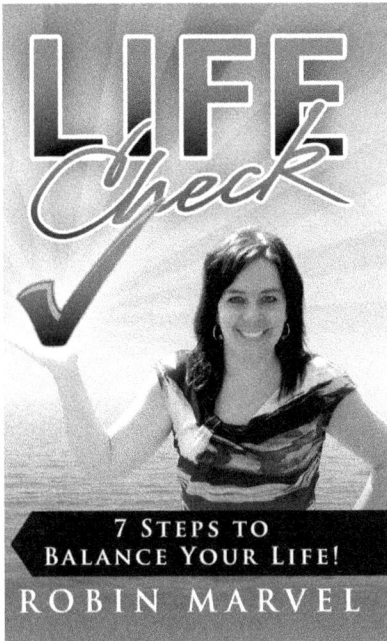

About Your Life:

- Do you keep asking yourself, when will I be happy?
- Have you forgot what it feels like to be passionate about your life?
- Do you allow excuses to become the reason you are not going after what you desire in your life?
- Do you feel you are worth an amazing life and deserve to get all the things that you desire?
- Have you been following the crowd so long you have lost sight of the real you?

If you answered yes to any of these questions, Life Check is the book for you!

Life Check provides simple, effective ways to balance your life. Encouraging you to stop asking what if and start living the life you have imagined. Freeing yourself from the mundane routine of life by providing life tools that will get you rocking the boat, diving in and finding your passion for being alive!

"*Life Check* is the perfect resource for motivation, inspiration, and a reassurance that the life we are looking for is clearly within our reach."

--Victor Schueller, Professor of Positivity and Possibility

"If you are seriously ready to make the changes necessary to create the authentic life you deserve and don't quite know where to begin, I urge you to read and implement the loving guidance contained in this easy to read, straightforward book."

--Rinnell Kelly, *Scents of Wellbeing*

ISBN-13: 978-1-61599-204-1
List Price: Paperback $14.95 / eBook $4.95

www.MarvelousSpirit.com